TREATS

just great recipes

GENERAL INFORMATION

The level of difficulty of the recipes in this book
is expressed as a number from 1 (simple) to 3 (difficult).

TREATS
just great recipes

eggs

McRae Books

SERVES 4

PREPARATION 5 min + 1 h to chill

DIFFICULTY level 1

Egg Dip

with crudities

Place the cream cheese in a medium bowl and stir in the mayonnaise, mustard, Worcestershire sauce, chives, eggs, and milk. Mix until smooth. • Season with salt and pepper and chill in the refrigerator for at least 1 hour. • Just before serving, rinse and scrape the carrots, then cut into strips. Remove any tough fibers from the celery and cut into strips the same size as the carrots. • Arrange the raw vegetables on a large platter. • Spoon the egg dip into an attractive serving dish and place at the center of the platter with the vegetables arranged around it.

8 oz (250 g) cream cheese
2 tablespoons mayonnaise
2 teaspoons spicy mustard
Salt and freshly ground white pepper
1 teaspoon Worcestershire sauce
1 tablespoon finely chopped fresh chives
2 large hard-boiled eggs
3 tablespoons milk
2 carrots
2 stalks celery

MAKES 2 cups (500 ml)

PREPARATION 10 min

DIFFICULTY level 2

Mayonnaise
with mustard and tarragon

Break the eggs into the bowl of a food processor, add the mustard, sugar, salt, pepper, and vinegar. • Blend briefly, then with the motor still running, add the oil very slowly at first and then in a steady stream. The mayonnaise will thicken suddenly. • If it is too stiff, beat in enough boiling water to create the right consistency. • Store in a covered jar in the refrigerator.

2 large eggs
3 level teaspoons French mustard
$\frac{1}{2}$ teaspoon sugar
Salt and freshly ground black pepper
2 tablespoons tarragon vinegar
2 cups (500 ml) sunflower oil

Stuffed Eggs
with fresh herbs

Cut the eggs in half lengthwise. • Scoop out the yolks, being careful not to break the whites. • Combine the yolks with the cream, herbs, mayonnaise, salt, and pepper and mash with a fork. • Use a teaspoon to stuff the filling into the hollow egg whites. Sprinkle each egg with a splash of paprika for extra color. • Arrange the salad greens on a serving dish. Place the eggs on the dish along with slices of tomato.

4 large hard-boiled eggs, shelled
2 tablespoons heavy (double) cream
2 tablespoons finely chopped mixed fresh herbs
1/4 cup (60 ml) mayonnaise
Salt and freshly ground black pepper
Dash of paprika
Salad greens and salad tomatoes, to serve

Egg Appetizer

Mix the basil, parsley, capers, and olives together in a medium bowl. Stir in the Parmesan and bread crumbs. Gradually stir in the wine. • Season with pepper and gradually stir in the oil. The mixture should be thick but still fluid. • Place the eggs on a platter with the yolks facing up. Spoon the mixture over the eggs and serve.

8 basil leaves, finely chopped

3 tablespoons finely chopped fresh parsley

2 tablespoons capers, finely chopped

5 oz (150 g) green olives, pitted and finely chopped

1 cup (125 g) freshly grated Parmesan cheese

$\frac{1}{2}$ cup (75 g) fine dry bread crumbs

$\frac{3}{4}$ cup (180 ml) dry white wine

Freshly ground black pepper

$\frac{1}{4}$ cup (60 ml) extra-virgin olive oil

12 large hard-boiled eggs, sliced in half lengthwise

Egg Toasts
with spinach cream

Preheat the oven to 350°F (180°C/gas 4). • Use a small glass or cookie cutter to cut 8 disks out of the bread. Brush with the oil and place on a baking sheet. Toast for 8–10 minutes, or until nicely browned. • Wash the spinach under cold running water. Do not drain but place in a saucepan and cook, with just the water clinging to its leaves, for 3 minutes. • Drain, press out the excess water, and place in a food processor. • Add the cream and Parmesan and process until smooth. Season with salt and pepper. • Use a teaspoon to remove the yolks from the eggs. Crumble and set aside. • Fill the eggs with the spinach cream. • Arrange the disks of toast on a serving dish. Place half an egg, filling-side up, on each toast. Sprinkle with the egg yolks and chives.

8 slices white sandwich bread

2 tablespoons extra-virgin olive oil

8 oz (250 g) fresh spinach leaves

$\frac{1}{2}$ cup (125 ml) heavy (double) cream

6 tablespoons freshly grated Parmesan cheese

Salt and freshly ground black pepper

4 large hard-boiled eggs, shelled

2 tablespoons finely chopped fresh chives

Stuffed Eggs
with zucchini

Sauté the zucchini, garlic, and basil in 2 tablespoons of oil in a large frying pan over medium heat until the garlic is pale gold. Season with salt and pepper. • Remove the yolks from the eggs and place in a food processor or blender with the zucchini mixture. Chop until smooth. • Fill the egg whites with the mixture. • Arrange the salad greens on a serving dish and place the filled eggs on top. • Sprinkle with the bell peppers and drizzle with the remaining oil. • Season with salt and pepper and serve.

12 oz (350 g) zucchini (courgettes), thinly sliced
1 clove garlic, lightly crushed but whole
4 tablespoons torn basil
$1/3$ cup (90 ml) extra-virgin olive oil
Salt and freshly ground black pepper
6 large hard-boiled eggs, shelled
1 bunch fresh salad greens
6 tablespoons diced mixed red and yellow bell peppers (capsicums)

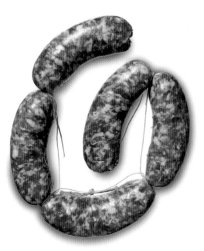

Scotch Eggs

Place the sausage meat in a large bowl with the parsley, chives, and tomato purée and mix well. • Season with salt and pepper. • Roll the hard-boiled eggs in the seasoned flour. • Divide the sausage meat mixture into four equal portions. • On a floured board, flatten each portion out into a piece large enough to wrap around an egg. Place the egg on a piece of sausage meat and carefully enclose it, overlapping at the seams. Smooth the seams, forming a neat oval and making sure that no egg is showing. • Repeat with the other eggs. • Finally, carefully dip the eggs in the beaten egg and roll them in the bread crumbs. • Heat the oil in a deep-fryer or deep frying pan until very hot. Test the oil by dropping a small piece of bread into it. When hot enough, the bread will turn brown instantly. • Fry the eggs in the oil for 6–8 minutes, until golden brown. • Drain on paper towels and serve hot or at room temperature.

8 oz (250 g) sausage meat
1 tablespoon finely chopped fresh parsley
1 teaspoon finely chopped fresh chives
1 tablespoon tomato purée (paste)
Salt and freshly ground black pepper
1 cup (150 g) all-purpose (plain) flour, seasoned with salt and pepper
4 large hard-boiled eggs, shelled
1 small egg, beaten
1/2 cup (75 g) fine dry bread crumbs
4 cups (1 liter) oil, for frying

SERVES 2–4

PREPARATION 20 min

COOKING 20–25 min

DIFFICULTY level I

Egg Curry
with basmati rice

Sauté the onion in the ghee in a large frying pan over medium heat until golden brown, 5–7 minutes. • Add the ginger, garlic, salt, garam masala, coriander seeds, and chile and sauté for 2 minutes. • Stir in the tomatoes and cook for 5 minutes. Add the cilantro. • Add the eggs and simmer over low heat for 5 minutes, or until the sauce thickens. • Serve hot with the rice.

1 large onion, finely chopped
1 tablespoon ghee (clarified butter)
1 piece ginger, finely chopped
2 cloves garlic, finely chopped
1 teaspoon salt
1 teaspoon garam masala
1 teaspoon coriander seeds, crushed
$\frac{1}{2}$ teaspoon chile powder
1 (14-oz/400-g) can tomatoes, with juice
1 small bunch fresh cilantro (coriander), finely chopped
6 hard-boiled eggs, peeled but whole
Freshly cooked basmati rice, to serve

SERVES 8

PREPARATION 10 min

COOKING 10 min

DIFFICULTY level 1

Scrambled Eggs
Mexican-style

Heat the oil in a large frying pan over medium heat. • Beat the eggs until frothy, then add the chilies, onion, cilantro, and salt. • Pour the mixture into the hot oil and cook until the eggs are softly scrambled, stirring them with a fork so they cook evenly. • Heat the beans gently over low heat. To serve, spoon the beans onto a deep platter and top with the scrambled eggs.

½ cup (125 ml) extra-virgin olive oil
16 large eggs
2 green jalapeño chilies, finely chopped
1 white onion, finely chopped
6 tablespoons finely chopped fresh
   cilantro (coriander)
Salt
3 cups (750 g) cooked black beans

Spicy Eggs
Thai-style

Bring the eggs to a boil in a saucepan and boil for 7 minutes. • Drain and rinse under cold running water. Shell the eggs and cut them in half lengthwise. • While the eggs are cooking, sauté the onions, chilies, ginger, cinnamon, and turmeric in the butter in a large frying pan over medium heat until the onions have softened, about 5 minutes. • Pour in the coconut milk and lemon juice. Season with salt and mix well. Carefully place the eggs, yolk-side up, in the sauce. Simmer over medium heat for 3 minutes, or until the sauce has thickened slightly. • Garnish with the lemon zest and serve hot.

4 large eggs
4 large onions, finely sliced
3 fresh red chilies, seeded and finely sliced
2 tablespoons finely grated fresh ginger
1/2 teaspoon ground cinnamon
1/2 teaspoon turmeric
1/4 cup (60 g) butter
1/2 cup (125 ml) coconut milk
3 tablespoons freshly squeezed lemon juice
Salt
Zest of 1/2 lemon, very finely cut, to garnish

SERVES 4
PREPARATION 10 min
COOKING 15 min
DIFFICULTY level 1

Scrambled Eggs
with cauliflower and pancetta

Cook the cauliflower in a large pot of salted, boiling water until just tender, 7–8 minutes. • Beat the eggs and cheese in a large bowl. Season with salt and pepper. • Sauté the pancetta and garlic in the oil in a large frying pan over medium heat until the garlic turns pale gold, about 3 minutes. • Add the cauliflower and mix well. Lower the heat and pour in the egg mixture. Cook for 2–3 minutes, stirring constantly, until the egg is cooked. • Serve hot.

1 medium cauliflower, cut into small florets
4 large eggs, lightly beaten
4 tablespoons freshly grated pecorino or Parmesan cheese
Salt and freshly ground black pepper
$\frac{1}{2}$ cup (60 g) diced pancetta
1 clove garlic, finely chopped
2 tablespoons extra-virgin olive oil

SERVES 4

PREPARATION 10 min

COOKING 15 min

DIFFICULTY level 1

Fiery Eggs

with cherry tomatoes

Sauté the onion and garlic in the oil in a large frying pan over medium heat until softened, about 5 minutes. • Stir in the tomatoes and chile. Season with salt and pepper. Cook for 2 minutes. • Break the eggs into the pan with the tomatoes. Cook until the whites are set but the yolks are still slightly runny, for 5–7 minutes. • Serve hot with freshly baked crusty bread.

1 onion, finely chopped

1/4 cup (60 ml) extra-virgin olive oil

1 clove garlic, finely chopped

2 lb (1 kg) cherry tomatoes, cut in half

1 fresh red or green chile, seeded and finely chopped

Salt and freshly ground black pepper

6 large eggs

Freshly baked crusty bread, to serve

Eggs au Gratin

Preheat the oven to 400°F (200°C/gas 6). • Oil an ovenproof baking dish. • Melt the butter in a medium saucepan over low heat. Add the flour and mix until smooth. • Pour in the milk, stirring constantly. Bring to a boil and remove from the heat. • Stir in half the Parmesan and nutmeg. • Arrange layers of the cheese sauce, Fontina, and eggs in the prepared dish, finishing with a layer of cheese sauce. Sprinkle with the remaining Parmesan. • Bake for 10–15 minutes, or until golden and bubbling. • Serve hot.

2 tablespoons butter
2 tablespoons all-purpose (plain) flour
2 cups (500 ml) milk
1 cup (125 g) freshly grated Parmesan cheese
1/4 teaspoon freshly grated nutmeg
8 oz (250 g) Fontina cheese, diced
8 hard-boiled eggs, thinly sliced

Cheese Soufflé

Preheat the oven to 350°F (180°C/gas 4). • Lightly beat the egg yolks in a large bowl. • Add the milk, butter, and mustard to the egg yolks and mix well. • Stir in the bread crumbs and cheese and season with the salt and pepper. • Beat the egg whites with a dash of salt until stiff. Fold into the yolk mixture. • Pour into a buttered soufflé dish. Bake for 30–40 minutes, or until well risen and brown on top and set in the middle. • Serve at once.

4 large eggs, separated
1¼ cups (300 ml) milk, warmed
1 tablespoon butter, melted
1 teaspoon mustard
3 oz (90 g) fresh bread crumbs
4 oz (125 g) Cheddar or Emmenthal cheese, grated
Salt and freshly ground black pepper

SERVES 4–6

PREPARATION 20 min

COOKING 15–20 min

DIFFICULTY level 2

Spinach Soufflé
with gorgonzola

Preheat the oven to 400°F (200°C/gas 6). • Oil six 1-cup (250-ml) soufflé molds or one 6-cup (1.5-liter) soufflé mold and sprinkle with bread crumbs. • Melt the butter in a medium saucepan over low heat. Add the flour and mix until smooth. • Pour in the milk, stirring constantly. Add the gorgonzola and bring to a boil stirring constantly. The gorgonzola should melt completely into the sauce. • Boil the spinach in lightly salted water until tender. • Drain and chop in a food processor until smooth. • Place in a bowl and stir in the ricotta, egg yolks, nutmeg, Parmesan, and Béchamel sauce. Season with salt and pepper. • Beat the egg whites until stiff peaks form. Fold them into the mixture. • Spoon the mixture into the prepared molds and bake until risen and golden brown, 15–20 minutes. • Serve hot.

2 tablespoons butter
2 tablespoons all-purpose (plain) flour
2 cups (500 ml) milk
5 oz (150 g) gorgonzola cheese, in small cubes
1/3 cup (50 g) fine dry bread crumbs
2 lb (1 kg) fresh spinach
1/2 cup (125 g) fresh ricotta, drained
3 large eggs, separated
Freshly grated nutmeg
4 tablespoons freshly grated Parmesan cheese
Salt and freshly ground white pepper

SERVES 4

PREPARATION 10 min

COOKING 20 min

DIFFICULTY level 1

Zucchini Frittata

Sauté the garlic in the oil in a large frying pan over medium heat until pale gold, about 3 minutes. • Add the zucchini and sauté until tender, 5–7 minutes. Season with salt and pepper. • Beat the eggs and cheese in a medium bowl. • Pour the egg mixture into the pan and cook until the egg is almost solid, 7–8 minutes. • Slide the frittata onto a plate, flip onto another plate, then slide it back into the pan to cook the other side. Cook until golden brown and the egg is cooked through. • Serve hot.

1 clove garlic, finely chopped

3 tablespoons extra-virgin olive oil

2 lb (1 kg) zucchini (courgettes), cut into short, thin lengths

Salt and freshly ground black pepper

6 large eggs

$\frac{1}{2}$ cup (60 g) freshly grated pecorino or Parmesan cheese

Plain Omelet

Beat the eggs, water, salt, and pepper briskly with a fork in a small bowl. • Drop the butter into an omelet pan and place over high heat. • When the butter is foaming, pour the eggs into the pan. • Start lifting the edges of the mixture around the pan with a fork to allow the runny, uncooked egg to get underneath. • Continue to do this until the omelet is set – it will only take a minute or two. • Slip the fork under one side, fold the omelet in half, and slide it onto a warmed plate. • Garnish with the parsley and serve hot.

2 large eggs
1 tablespoon cold water
Salt and freshly ground pepper
1 tablespoon butter
sprig of parsley to garnish

Omelet
with ham and cheese

Beat the egg yolks, water, and lemon juice with an electric mixer at high speed in a medium bowl until pale. Season with salt and pepper. • With mixer at high speed, beat the egg whites in a large bowl until stiff peaks form. • Use a large rubber spatula to fold the egg yolk mixture into the beaten whites. • Melt the butter in a large frying pan over medium heat. Pour the egg mixture into the pan and cook for 3–4 minutes, or until the egg is almost set. • Sprinkle with the ham and Gruyère. Use a spatula to fold the omelet in half. Cook for 2–3 minutes more, or until golden brown and the egg is cooked through. • Serve hot.

5 large eggs, separated
2 teaspoons water
2 teaspoons freshly squeezed lemon juice
Salt and freshly ground black pepper
1 tablespoon butter
$\frac{3}{4}$ cup (100 g) diced ham
1 cup (125 g) freshly grated Gruyère cheese

SERVES 4

PREPARATION 10 min

COOKING 30 min

DIFFICULTY level 2

Potato Frittata

with hams and peas

Heat 2 tablespoons of oil in a large frying pan over low heat. Add the sliced onions and sauté for 3 minutes, until they begin to soften. • Add the potatoes and sauté until soft, 5–10 minutes. Season with salt and pepper. • Add the thyme and mix well. Transfer to a bowl and let cool. • Chop the remaining onion. • Heat 2 tablespoons of the oil in a frying pan over medium heat. Add the onion and sauté for 3 minutes, until it begins to soften. • Add the ham and the peas. Sauté until the peas are tender, 5–7 minutes. Season with salt and pepper. Remove from the heat. • Beat the eggs in a bowl. Add the Parmesan and season with salt and pepper. • Pour over the potatoes and mix well. Add the peas and ham and mix well. • Heat the remaining oil in a large frying pan over medium heat. Pour the potato mixture into the pan and cook for 6–8 minutes, until the egg is almost set. • Slide the frittata onto a plate, flip onto another plate, then back into the pan. Cook the other side until golden brown, 3–4 minutes. • Garnish with parsley and serve hot.

$^1/_3$ cup (90 ml) extra-virgin olive oil

3 small onions, 2 finely sliced

$1^1/_2$ lb (750 g) waxy potatoes, peeled and thinly sliced

Salt and freshly ground black pepper

1 tablespoon finely chopped fresh thyme

3 oz (90 g) cooked ham, chopped

$1^1/_4$ cups (200 g) fresh or frozen peas

4 large eggs

$^1/_2$ cup (60 g) freshly grated Parmesan cheese

SERVES 4

PREPARATION 10 min

COOKING 20 min

DIFFICULTY level 1

Poached Eggs
with spinach

Cook the spinach in a medium pot of salted boiling water until just tender, about 5 minutes. • Drain and squeeze out excess moisture. Season the spinach with salt and chop finely. • Spoon the spinach into 4 small baking dishes or ramekins. Make a hollow in the center of each portion. Break an egg into the hollows and top each one with 1 tablespoon of cream. Season with salt and pepper. • Place the baking dishes in a large saucepan and pour in hot water to halfway up the sides of the ramekins. Bring the water to a gentle Cover and simmer until the eggs have set, 10–15 minutes. • Serve hot.

1 lb (500 g) frozen spinach
Salt and freshly ground black pepper
4 large eggs
1/4 cup (60 ml) heavy (double) cream

Asparagus Gratin

with bacon

Preheat the oven to 300°F (150°C/gas 2). • Cook the asparagus in salted, boiling water until tender, 5–10 minutes. Drain well, reserving the cooking water. • Sauté the bacon lightly and set aside. • Melt the butter in a small saucepan and add the flour and mustard powder. Stir for a few minutes over medium heat. • Make the milk up to 2 cups (500 ml) with the reserved asparagus water and slowly add to the saucepan, stirring steadily. • Season with salt and pepper. Stir in half the cheese and cook for 2–3 minutes. • Arrange the asparagus in an ovenproof dish. • Cut the hard-boiled eggs into quarters and place around the asparagus. • Scatter with the bacon and pour the sauce over the top. • Mix the remaining cheese with the bread crumbs and scatter over the surface. • Bake for 25–30 minutes, until golden brown. Serve hot.

1 bunch asparagus, trimmed

2 large thin slices of bacon, cut into small pieces

1½ tablespoons butter

¼ cup (30 g) all-purpose (plain) flour

½ teaspoon mustard powder

1 cup (250 ml) milk, warmed

4 oz (125 g) Cheddar cheese, freshly grated

Salt and freshly ground black pepper

6 large hard-boiled eggs, shelled

2 tablespoons fine dry bread crumbs

Fried Eggs

with potatoes and scallions

Put the potatoes in a medium saucepan and cover with water. Bring to a boil over medium heat. Simmer for 5 minutes. Drain well. • Heat the oil in a large frying pan over medium heat. Add the scallions and potatoes. Sauté for 5 minutes, taking care not to break the potatoes. Season with salt. • Make space around the edges of the pan for the eggs using a spatula. Break the eggs into the pan and cook for 4 minutes, until the eggs are cooked and the potatoes are tender. Season the eggs with salt. • Dust with the paprika and serve hot.

4 large waxy potatoes, peeled and sliced 1/4-inch (5-mm) thick
1/4 cup (60 ml) extra-virgin olive oil
6 scallions (spring onions), chopped
Salt
4 large eggs
Pinch of hot paprika

SERVES 4

PREPARATION 25 min

COOKING 45–50 min

DIFFICULTY level 2

Baked Frittata

with tomatoes and olives

Preheat the oven to 400°F (200°C/gas 6). • Place the bell peppers and tomatoes on a plate in a microwave oven. Cook at high heat for 3 minutes. Peel both vegetables. • Cut the bell peppers into strips and the tomatoes into wedges. • Sauté the onions in the oil in a large frying pan over low heat for about 10 minutes, or until softened. • Add the tomatoes, bell peppers, and herbs. Season with salt. • Cook for 5 minutes. Transfer to a bowl. • Beat the eggs, milk, and Gruyère in a large bowl. Pour into the fried vegetables. • Pour the mixture into a baking dish and garnish with the black olives. • Bake for 25–30 minutes, or until set and golden on top. • Serve hot or at room temperature.

2 red bell peppers (capsicums)
2 lb (1 kg) tomatoes
4 small onions, thinly sliced
3 tablespoons extra-virgin olive oil
1 small bunch aromatic herbs (oregano, basil, thyme, chervil), finely chopped
Salt
4 large eggs
1/2 cup (125 ml) milk
1 3/4 cups (200 g) freshly grated Gruyère cheese
1 cup (100 g) black olives, pitted

SERVES 4

PREPARATION 20 min

COOKING 15 min

DIFFICULTY level 3

Frittata Roll

with peas and pine nuts

Boil the peas in a small pan of lightly salted water. Drain well. • Beat the eggs in a large bowl. Add the bread crumbs, pecorino, and chives. Season with salt and pepper. • Heat 2 tablespoons of oil in a large frying pan over medium heat. Add the egg mixture and cook until golden brown underneath. • Remove from the heat and place a plate over the pan. Flip the pan so that the frittata is on the plate then slide it back into the pan, cooked side up. Cook until the other side is golden brown. • Heat the remaining oil in a small frying pan over high heat and sauté the peas, pine nuts, and thyme for 3–4 minutes. • When the frittata is cooked, place on a cutting board and spread with the pea and pine nut mixture. Sprinkle with the Parmesan and drizzle with the lemon juice. • Roll the frittata up carefully, slice, and serve hot.

1 cup (150 g) frozen peas

6 large eggs

1 cup (150 g) fine dry bread crumbs

2/3 cup (100 g) freshly grated pecorino cheese

2 tablespoons finely chopped fresh chives

Salt and freshly ground black pepper

1/4 cup (60 ml) extra-virgin olive oil

2 tablespoons pine nuts

1 tablespoon finely chopped fresh thyme

4 tablespoons freshly grated Parmesan cheese

1 tablespoon freshly squeezed lemon juice

Artichoke Frittata

If using fresh artichokes, trim the tops and remove the tough outer leaves. Trim the stalk. Cut in thin wedges, removing any fuzzy choke with a sharp knife, and drizzle with lemon juice. • Coat the artichoke pieces or thawed hearts with flour, shaking off any excess. • Heat all but 2 tablespoons of the oil in a large frying pan over high heat. • Fry the artichokes until lightly browned, 8–10 minutes. Drain on paper towels. • Discard the oil used for frying and replace with the remaining oil. Put the artichokes in the pan and return to medium-high heat. • Beat the eggs lightly with the salt and pepper and pour over the artichokes. Cook until the eggs have set and the underside is lightly browned, about 5 minutes. • To turn the frittata, place a large plate over the pan, turn it upside down and then slide the egg mixture back into the pan, browned side up. Cook until the bottom is browned, 3–4 minutes. • Serve hot.

8 small artichokes, or 16 frozen artichoke hearts, thawed
Freshly squeezed juice of 1 lemon
$1/3$ cup (50 g) all-purpose (plain) flour
$1/2$ cup (125 ml) extra-virgin olive oil
5 large eggs
Salt and freshly ground black pepper

SERVES 4

PREPARATION 20 min

COOKING 40–45 min

DIFFICULTY level 1

Baked Frittata
with potatoes and mushrooms

Cook the potatoes in a large pot of salted, boiling water until tender, about 25 minutes. Drain and slice thinly. • Preheat the oven to 350°F (180°C/gas 4). Butter an 8-inch (20-cm) baking pan. • Sauté the onion in the oil and butter in a large frying pan over medium heat until softened, 3–4 minutes. Add the mushrooms and herbs. Season with salt and pepper and simmer until the mushrooms are tender, 5–7 minutes. • Beat the eggs and cream in a medium bowl. Season with salt and pepper. Add the mushroom mixture and potatoes and mix well. • Place in the prepared baking pan. Bake until golden brown and set, 15–20 minutes. • Serve hot.

14 oz (400 g) potatoes, peeled
1 small onion, finely chopped
3 tablespoons extra-virgin olive oil
1 tablespoon butter
4 small porcini or white mushrooms, thinly sliced
1 tablespoon finely chopped fresh thyme
1 tablespoon finely chopped fresh marjoram
1 tablespoon finely chopped fresh parsley
1/2 tablespoon finely chopped fresh rosemary
Salt and freshly ground black pepper
4 large eggs
7 tablespoons heavy (double) cream

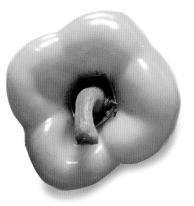

SERVES 4

PREPARATION 20 min

COOKING 25 min

DIFFICULTY level 1

Frittata
with bell peppers

Sauté the bell peppers and onion in the oil in a large earthenware dish or frying pan over medium heat until tender, about 10 minutes. • Stir in the tomatoes and basil. Season with salt. • Beat the eggs in a medium bowl until frothy. Season with salt. • Pour the eggs into the frying pan. Stir well and cook until the eggs have set. • Turn on the broiler (grill) and broil the frittata for 3–4 minutes, or until the top is golden. • Serve hot.

14 oz (400 g) mixed bell peppers (capsicums), seeded, cored, and coarsely chopped

1 onion, thinly sliced

2 tablespoons extra-virgin olive oil

14 oz (400 g) cherry tomatoes, coarsely chopped

4 leaves fresh basil, torn

Salt

6 large eggs

SERVES 2–4

PREPARATION 45 min + 1 h to rest

COOKING 30 min

DIFFICULTY level 2

Baked Crêpes
with ham and brie

Crêpes: Beat the egg yolks and salt in a bowl. • Beat in the flour until smooth. • Gradually pour in the milk, stirring constantly to prevent lumps from forming. • Beat the egg whites in a separate bowl until stiff. Fold them into the mixture. • Cover with plastic wrap (cling film) and let rest for 1 hour. • Melt 3 tablespoons of butter in a small frying pan and pour the butter into the batter. • Melt 1 tablespoon of butter in an 8-inch (20-cm) frying pan. Place a quarter of the batter in the pan. Rotate the pan so that it covers the bottom in an even layer. Place over medium heat and cook until the bottom is golden. • Flip the crêpe and brown on the other side. • Continue until all the batter is used. • Filling: Preheat the oven to 350°F (180°C/ gas 4). • Place 3 slices of ham on each crêpe. Top with 2 slices of brie and sprinkle with chives. • Fold the crêpes into triangles and place in a baking dish, overlapping them slightly. • Bake until the cheese melts, about 15 minutes. • Serve hot.

Crêpes
3 large eggs, separated
1/8 teaspoon salt
2 1/3 cups (350 g) all-purpose (plain) flour
2 cups (500 ml) milk
5 tablespoons butter

Filling
12 slices ham
8 slices brie
2 teaspoons finely chopped fresh chives

SERVES 4–6

PREPARATION 30 min + 1 h to rest

COOKING 1 h

DIFFICULTY level 2

Baked Crêpes

with with broccoli and fontina

Prepare the batter for the crêpes. Let rest for 1 hour. • Cook the crêpes and set aside in a warm place. • Preheat the oven to 400°F (200°C/ gas 6). • Oil a baking dish. • Filling: Melt the butter in a medium saucepan over low heat. Add the flour and mix until smooth. • Pour in the milk, stirring constantly, and stir until thickened, about 5 minutes. Season with salt and pepper. Remove from the heat. • Boil the broccoli in a medium saucepan of lightly salted water until just tender, about 5 minutes. Drain well. • Spread half the cream sauce on the crêpes. Fold them over and placed in the prepared baking dish. • Top with the broccoli and remaining cream sauce. • Bake until golden brown, about 10 minutes. Serve hot.

1 recipe crêpes (see page 44)

Filling
2 tablespoons butter
2 tablespoons all-purpose (plain) flour
2 cups (500 ml) milk
Salt and freshly ground black pepper
1 lb (500 g) broccoli, in florets
8 oz (250 g) freshly grated Fontina cheese

SERVES 4

PREPARATION 10–15 min

COOKING 15–20 min

DIFFICULTY level 1

Baked Omelet

with herbs

Preheat the oven to 400°F (200°C/gas 6). Grease a medium-sized ovenproof dish with the butter. • Place the ham and tomatoes in the dish and bake for 4–5 minutes. • Break the eggs into a bowl, add the cream or milk, salt, pepper, and herbs and beat lightly. • Take the dish out of the oven and carefully pour the egg mixture over the ham and tomatoes. • Bake for 15–20 minutes, until set. • Serve hot.

2 tablespoons butter, melted

3 oz (90 g) ham, finely chopped

2 tomatoes, peeled and sliced

6 large eggs

½ cup (125 ml) cream or milk

Salt and freshly ground black pepper

2 tablespoons mixed fresh herbs, finely chopped (chives, cilantro, parsley, oregano, basil, or other)

SERVES 4

PREPARATION 10 min

COOKING 25 min

DIFFICULTY level 1

Baked Frittata
with radicchio

Preheat the oven to 350°F (180°C/gas 4). • Beat the eggs in a large bowl. Season with salt and pepper. • Add the Parmesan and milk and beat well. • Heat the oil in a large frying pan over medium heat. Add the radicchio and sauté until tender, about 5 minutes. • Transfer to the bowl with the egg mixture and mix well. • Pour into an oiled baking dish. Bake until set and golden brown, about 20 minutes. • Run the blade of a knife around the edge of the dish and turn the frittata out onto a cutting board. • Cut it into squares and serve hot or at room temperature.

8 large eggs
Salt and freshly ground black pepper
$\frac{1}{2}$ cup (60 g) freshly grated Parmesan cheese
$\frac{1}{3}$ cup (90 ml) milk
$\frac{1}{4}$ cup (60 ml) extra-virgin olive oil
2 small heads radicchio, shredded

Baked Crêpes
with meatballs

Meat Sauce: Heat the oil in a large saucepan over high heat. Add the beef, sausage, and ham and cook until browned all over, 5–7 minutes. • Pour in the wine and let it evaporate. • Stir in the tomatoes and season with salt and pepper. Simmer over low heat for 1 hour. • Prepare the batter for the crêpes. Let rest for 1 hour. • Meatballs: Mix the veal, eggs, and pecorino in a medium bowl. Season with salt and pepper and form into balls the size of marbles. • Place the meatballs in the meat sauce and cook for 10 minutes. • Cook the crêpes. • Preheat the oven to 400°F (200°C/gas 6). • Grease a baking dish with oil and lay a crêpe on the bottom. Cover with a little of the meat sauce. Sprinkle with pieces of mozzarella, eggs, peas, and pecorino. Continue to layer until all the ingredients have been used. Dot with the butter and sprinkle with any remaining pecorino. • Bake until golden brown, 35–40 minutes. • Serve hot.

Meat Sauce

2 tablespoons extra-virgin olive oil

8 oz (200 g) lean ground (minced) beef

2 sausages, crumbled

4 oz (125 g) ham, finely chopped

1/3 cup (90 ml) dry red wine

2 cups (500 ml) canned tomatoes, with juice

Salt and freshly ground black pepper

1 recipe crêpes (see page 44)

Meatballs

12 oz (350 g) lean ground (minced) beef

2 large eggs

2 tablespoons freshly grated pecorino cheese

Filling

2 oz (60 g) mozzarella cheese, cut into cubes

2 hard-boiled eggs, thinly sliced

1/2 cup (75 g) frozen peas

1 cup (125 g) freshly grated pecorino cheese

1/4 cup (60 g) butter

SERVES 6

PREPARATION 5 min

COOKING 10 min

DIFFICULTY level 2

Basil Frittata

Beat the eggs in a large bowl. Add the cheese and season with salt and pepper. Add the basil and mix well. • Heat the oil in a large frying pan over medium heat. Pour the egg mixture into the pan and cook until the bottom is browned. • Slide the frittata onto a plate, flip it onto another plate, and turn slide it back into the pan. Cook until the egg is cooked through and lightly browned all over, 3–4 minutes. • Transfer to a serving dish. Garnish with basil and serve hot.

12 large eggs

1 cup (120 g) freshly grated pecorino or Parmesan cheese

Salt and freshly ground black pepper

Bunch of fresh basil, coarsely chopped + extra leaves, to garnish

2 tablespoons extra-virgin olive oil

SERVES 4

PREPARATION 30 min + 30 min to chill

COOKING 2 h 30 min

DIFFICULTY level 3

Pea Soufflés

Cook the peas in a large pot of salted, boiling water until tender. • Drain, place in a food processor, and chop until smooth. • Melt the butter in a small saucepan and stir in the flour. • Gradually stir in the milk and bring to a boil. Cook, stirring constantly over low heat, for 10 minutes. Season with salt. • Stir the sauce and Parmesan into the pea mixture and let cool. • Refrigerate for 30 minutes. • Preheat the oven to 400°F (200°C/gas 6). • Butter and flour 4 individual soufflé molds. • Beat the egg whites with a pinch of salt until stiff peaks form. Beat in the sugar. • Gently fold the egg whites into the pea mixture. Spoon the mixture into the prepared molds. • Bake for 12–15 minutes, or until golden brown on top. • Serve hot.

1½ cups (200 g) fresh or frozen peas
2 tablespoons butter
2 tablespoons all-purpose (plain) flour
1 cup (250 ml) milk
Salt
2 tablespoons freshly grated Parmesan cheese
6 large egg whites
1 tablespoon sugar

Zabaione

Combine the egg yolks and sugar in the top of a double boiler (not on the heat yet) and whisk until pale yellow and creamy. • Add the Marsala gradually, beating continuously, then place over barely simmering water and cook, beating continuously with the whisk, until the mixture thickens, 10–15 minutes. Do not allow the zabaione to boil or it will curdle. • Serve warm or cold. If serving cold, cover with plastic wrap (cling film) so that it is touching the surface to prevent a skin from forming as the mixture cools.

4 large egg yolks
1/4 cup (50 g) superfine (caster) sugar
1/3 cup (90 ml) dry Marsala wine
   (or sherry)

Coconut Custard

Preheat the oven to 325°F (170°C/gas 3). • Put the eggs, yolk, sugar, and almond extract in a large bowl and beat well. • Warm the coconut milk with the cream or milk to blood heat. • Slowly pour this mixture onto the eggs, whisking continuously. • Pour into an ovenproof dish. Place the dish in a roasting pan. Pour in enough water to come halfway up the outside of the dish. • Bake for 1 hour, or until the custard is set. • Serve warm or chilled.

3 large eggs + 1 large egg yolk
1/4 cup (50 g) sugar
1/2 teaspoon almond extract (essence)
2 cups (500 ml) coconut milk
1 1/4 cups (150 ml) cream or milk

SERVES 6

PREPARATION 1 h

COOKING 40 min

DIFFICULTY level 2

Meringue Roll
with kiwi fruit

Preheat the oven to 350°F (180°C/gas 4). Grease a 10 x 6½ inch (26 x 16-cm) baking pan and line it with parchment paper. • Beat the egg whites with an electric mixer on high speed until stiff. • Add the sugar gradually, beating continuously until the mixture is thick. • Fold in the confectioners' sugar and cornstarch and beat again briefly. • Stir in the vinegar. • Spread the mixture in the prepared baking pan and smooth the surface. • Bake for 30 minutes. • Cool in the baking pan. • Turn the roll out onto parchment paper and carefully peel off the paper. • Spread with the whipped cream and cover with the kiwi fruit. • Roll up like a jelly roll (Swiss roll) and serve.

3 large egg whites
¾ cup (150 g) sugar
1 tablespoon confectioners' (icing) sugar, sifted
1 teaspoon cornstarch (cornflour)
½ teaspoon white wine vinegar
2 kiwi fruit, peeled and sliced
1¼ cups (300 ml) heavy (double) cream, whipped

SERVES 8–10

PREPARATION 45 min

COOKING 45 min

DIFFICULTY level 3

Floating Islands

Vanilla Custard: Beat the egg yolks and sugar in a large bowl with an electric mixer at high speed until pale and thick. • Bring the milk to a boil in a small saucepan with the vanilla beans. • Gradually pour the milk over the beaten yolk mixture. Beat for 2 minutes. • Return the mixture to the saucepan and cook over low heat, beating constantly until the mixture lightly coats a metal spoon or registers 160°F (70°C) on an instant-read thermometer. Remove from the heat and beat for 2–3 minutes more. The custard should be very liquid. • Floating Islands: Beat the egg whites and salt with an electric mixer at high speed until soft peaks form. Gradually add 2 cups (400 g) of sugar, beating until stiff peaks form. • Bring the 3 quarts (3 liters) of water to a boil in a large saucepan. Turn the heat down to very low and pour in 1 cup (250 ml) cold water to stop it boiling. • Use 2 dessert spoons to form balls of meringue about the size of golf balls. Plunge them into the water to poach for 2 minutes. Use a slotted spoon to turn over and poach for 2 minutes on the other side. Remove from the water and place on a clean cloth. • Heat the candied fruit in the rum in a small saucepan for 2–3 minutes. Remove from heat and, if the fruit is sticking together, divide it into single pieces. • Place the remaining sugar in a heavy-bottomed saucepan with the ½ cup (125 ml) of water and cook until a liquid caramel has formed. • Pour the custard into a large serving dish. Place the meringues on top and drizzle with the caramel. Sprinkle with the candied fruit and almonds.

Vanilla Custard
8 large egg yolks
1 cup (200 g) sugar
2 quarts (2 liters) milk
2 vanilla beans, cut in half, or 1 teaspoon vanilla extract

Floating Islands
16 large eggs, separated
¼ teaspoon salt
4 cups (800 g) sugar
2 tablespoons lukewarm milk
3 quarts (3 liters) + 1 cup cold water, + ½ cup (125 ml) for the caramel sauce
1 cup (100 g) candied fruit, cut into small cubes
1 tablespoon dark rum
½ cup (50 g) flaked almonds

Meringue Cake
with raspberries and cream

Preheat the oven to 200°F (100°C). • Cut out three 9-inch (23-cm) disks of parchment paper and place on two baking sheets. Cut one 8 x 12-inch (20 x 32-cm) rectangle of parchment paper and place on one of the baking sheets. • Beat the egg whites and salt in a large bowl with an electric mixer at medium speed until frothy. • With mixer at high speed, gradually add the superfine sugar, beating until stiff, glossy peaks form. • Spread a quarter of the meringue onto each of the three parchment disks. Spoon the remaining meringue onto the rectangle of parchment paper to make 6–8 small meringues to decorate the cake. • Bake with the oven door ajar for 50–60 minutes so that the meringue does not turn brown. Remove the small meringues and continue baking for 10–15 minutes, or until crisp. Turn the oven off and let the meringues cool in the oven with the door ajar. Remove from the oven and carefully remove the paper. • With mixer at high speed, beat the cream, confectioners' sugar, and vanilla in a large bowl until stiff. • Place one meringue round on a serving plate. Spread with one-third of the cream and sprinkle with one-third of the raspberries. Top with another meringue round. Spread with one-third of the cream and sprinkle with one-third of the raspberries. Top with another round and spread with the cream. Decorate with the remaining raspberries and the small meringues.

9 large egg whites
1/8 teaspoon salt
3 cups (600 g) superfine (caster) sugar
3 cups (750 ml) heavy (double) cream
1/3 cup (50 g) confectioners' (icing) sugar
1 teaspoon vanilla extract (essence)
2 cups (300 g) fresh raspberries

Index

Eggs

was created and produced by McRae Books Srl

Borgo Santa Croce, 8 – Florence (Italy)

info@mcraebooks.com

Publishers: Anne McRae and Marco Nardi

Project Director: Anne McRae

Design: Sara Mathews

Text: McRae Books archive

Editing: Carla Bardi

Photography: Studio Lanza (Lorenzo Borri, Cristina Canepari, Ke-ho Casati, Mauro Corsi, Gil Gallo, Leonardo Pasquinelli, Gianni Petronio, Stefano Pratesi, Sandra Preussinger)

Home Economist: Benedetto Rillo

Artbuying: McRae Books

Layouts: Aurora Granata, Filippo Delle Monache, Davide Gasparri

Repro: Fotolito Raf, Florence

ISBN 978-88-6098-076-2

Printed and bound in China